For Parents

First, thank you!

We at Tappity understand the significance of choosing a platform to educate your child in crucial science concepts. We take this responsibility to heart and are committed to delivering the highest quality of both physical and digital learning experiences for your family.

If at any point our offerings do not **exceed** your expectations, please don't hesitate to reach out and let us know. We're dedicated to continually improving and are here to support you in ensuring your homeschooling journey is as successful as possible.

How to use this book

This book is created to be paired with the Tappity digital 2nd grade science course. Each lesson in this book is designed to be completed during live classes (also available as on-demand recordings) or with video guides to check your work on your learning path page.

Useful book tips

At the top of each page, you will see the following visual keys to help you navigate within the book.

📖 **C 2 L 1**   C & L refers to chapter & lesson. Use this to find the corresponding video lesson.

💻 **During-Class**   If the page is to be completed during or after a live class.

🔍 **Properties of Materials**   The main concept covered on the page.

✖️ **Hands-on Activity**   The type of activity on the page.

💡   We call attention to important definitions or concepts with this symbol.

🖌️   We keep required materials limited to what families tend to have around the house. Activities that require materials will have this symbol at the top.

Customer support

Monday-Friday 8am-6pm PST
(415) 320-6038

Hey@TappityApp.com

Science Standards and Concepts

Next Generation Science Standards (NGSS)

The Next Generation Science Standards is a multi-state effort to create a comphrensive set of science standards for K-12 students in the United States and are a great starting point for a science curriculum. Over 20 states have voluntarily adopted NGSS. We combine these standards with what children are curious about, current world events, and practical skills to provide a modern well-rounded science curriculum that prepares children for anything they might want to pursue.

You can learn more about these standards on our website:
www.stemschool.tappityapp.com/2nd-grade-science-education-outline

Concepts & topics covered

ENGINEERING

Think like an engineer

How to invent

Define a problem

Build a strong structure

Invent a unique hat

Invent a new material

How scientists use models

Test with models

Scientific method

MATERIALS SCIENCE

Properties of materials

Insulator vs conductor

States of matter

State change reversal

PLANTS

Plant needs

Greenhouses

Plant adaptation

Seed dispersal

Plant biodiversity

EARTH'S SURFACE

Erosion

How rivers/lakes form

Glacial lakes

Tectonic lakes

Land formations

Geologic time

Landslides

Natural disaster prevention

ANIMALS

Animal classification

Animal adaptation

Vertebrates

Invertebrates

Fish

Mammals

Reptiles

Birds

Amphibians

Animal biodiversity

Local nature

Bird feeder science

Animal vs plant

Species variation

Chapter 1
Think Like An Engineer

 Chapter Summary

In this chapter, we'll explore different materials and how to evaluate their unique properties. We'll see how they can help us solve real-world problems and invent useful things. Throughout this course, we will apply this engineering knowledge to the scientific domains of plants, landscapes, and animals.

Next Generation Science Standards covered
2-PS1-1, 2-PS1-2, K-2-ETS1-1, K-2-ETS1-2, K-2-ETS1-3, 2-PS1-1, 2-PS1-2, 2-PS1-3, 2-PS1-4, 2-PS1-1

What is a Good Conductor of Heat?

Follow along and circle the materials that are good at conducting heat.

 A material is a good **conductor of heat** if it is good at **transferring heat**. Example: Metal spoons are good conductors because they transfer heat from your hot soup to your hand.

Q: What materials do you think these homes are made of?

A: These homes are made of adobe which is a combination of earth, water, straw, and other natural materials. It's great at keeping homes cool.

Which Home Would Be Hotter Inside On a Sunny Day and Why?

Wood home

Metal home

Design Your Own Hat!

Think about the problems your hat solves and what materials are best for solving those problems. Label the special features and materials you would use.

 Humans **invent things to solve problems** or make life more fun! Think about what problems your hat might solve or how it might make life more fun.

Q: What material do sheep produce?

Sheep grow wool as a natural coat to keep warm and safe from the weather. People shear the wool off sheep (it doesn't hurt them!) and turn it into yarn. This yarn is used to make things like sweaters and blankets because wool is really good at keeping you warm, it's breathable, and even fire-resistant. So, wool is a pretty awesome material for both sheep and humans!

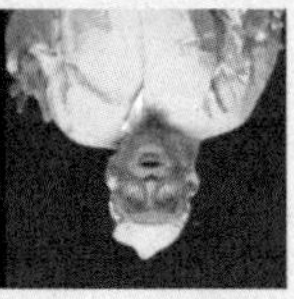

Insulator or Conductor?

Circle the best insulating material in each group.

 A good **insulator of heat** does not easily let heat pass through it. An insulator can keep a room warm by trapping heat inside or keep it cool by blocking heat from getting inside.

Circle the best insulator:

Circle the best insulator:

Circle the best insulator:

Meltable Materials

Circle the materials that you could easily melt.

 Meltable materials like ice or chocolate can change from a solid to a liquid when it gets warmer, and that's called **changing their state of matter**!

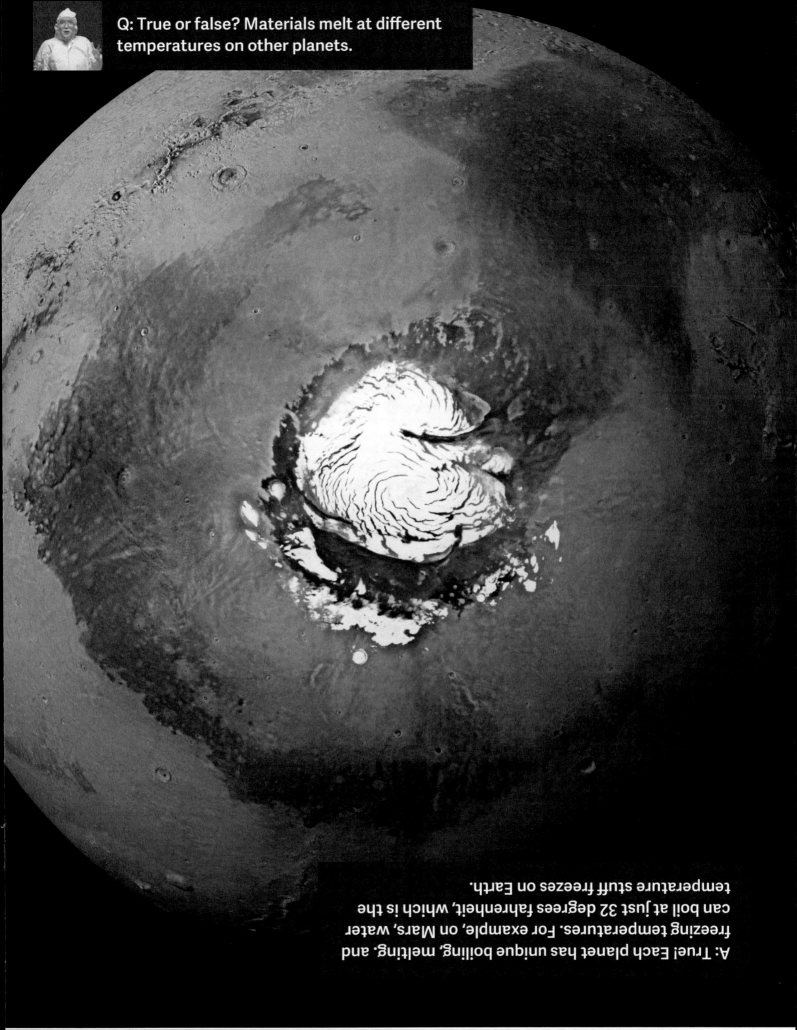

Q: True or false? Materials melt at different temperatures on other planets.

A: True! Each planet has unique boiling, melting, and freezing temperatures. For example, on Mars, water can boil at just 32 degrees Fahrenheit, which is the temperature stuff freezes on Earth.

State Change Reversal

Think about each state change and if it can be reversed.

Some changes caused by heating or cooling can be reversed and some cannot. Water, for example, can be turned into a solid and easily turned back into a liquid by heating it up.

Can melted ice cream be turned back into solid ice cream? How? Would it be different?

_____

_____

_____

Can a melted ice cube be turned back into a solid cube? How? Would it be different?

_____

_____

_____

Can a melted plastic toy turn back into a solid? Would it look different?

_____

_____

_____

Hunt for Different Materials

Find and describe different materials in your house or outside.

 A **property of a material** is something special about it that helps us know what it can do. Examples of properties are strength, flexibility, hardness, texture, and absorbency.

Find a meltable material

Draw it below and describe it on the right.

Is it soft or hard?

Is it flexible?

What other properties does it have?

Find a lightweight material

Draw it below and describe it on the right.

Is it soft or hard?

Does it absorb water?

What other properties does it have?

Living in Kenya, 11-year-old Richard Turere devised a system of flashing lights to scare away lions from his family's livestock enclosure. The invention, known as "Lion Lights," helped protect both the livestock and the endangered lions, which are often killed in retaliation for attacking livestock.

Chapter Review

Answer these questions as best you can.

1. Circle the object that is a better conductor of heat...

2. Why do humans invent things?

3. What problems would you face if you built a home out of chocolate?

4. Which of these is not a property of materials? Circle your answer.

A. How strong it is

B. How easily it melts

C. What color it is

D. All of these are properties of a material

Q: True or false. There are materials that can "remember" their shape.

A: True! These are called "shape-memory alloys," and they can go back to their original shape when you heat them up! Imagine bending a spoon made of this material, and then watching it magically straighten itself out when you dip it in hot water!

This cool property is used in all kinds of things, from eyeglass frames that snap back into shape if you accidentally sit on them, to special medical devices that help heal people's hearts!

Parent Review

Discussion questions

1. What does it mean if a material is a good conductor of heat? *(Answer: It's good at transferring heat. A good example is how the entire metal spoon gets hot if you leave it in a pot of hot soup.)*

2. Pick a material or object in the house. Ask your child to list its properties. You can guide them by asking if it's strong, soft, flexible, etc.

3. What are some problems you face that we could invent solutions for?

Parent sign-off

☑ During-Class Pages ☐ After-Class Pages ☐ Discussion Questions

✕ _____ Parent signature

💡 Don't worry about completing activities if they aren't useful/doable for your family. Your child can always follow along with them in our video recordings.

 Materials needed for this chapter: 20+ paper index cards. Objects like a book or apple to test how much weight your structure can hold.

Chapter 2

Become An Engineer

 Chapter Summary

In this chapter, students complete their introduction to thinking like an engineer. Students will continue to learn new properties of materials and decide how these characteristics might help solve problems. In class, they will invent their own material, describe its properties, and explain why it is uniquely capable of solving a problem.

Materials needed for live class
Please bring ~20 index cards to class.

Next Generation Science Standards covered
2-PS1-1, 2-PS1-2, K-2-ETS1-1, K-2-ETS1-2, K-2-ETS1-3, 2-PS1-1, 2-PS1-2, 2-PS1-3, 2-PS1-4, 2-PS1-1

You can shape index cards so they are more useful to build with.

This is a strong structure.

This is a tall structure.

Paper Structures
Design and build different structures out of index cards.

Build a tall structure
Draw what your tall structure looks like.

How did you make your structure stand tall?

Build a strong structure
Draw what your strong structure looks like.

How did you make your structure stronger? Can it hold a book?

Strong & Durable Materials

Circle the items below that are both strong and durable.

 If something is **durable** it is able to withstand wear, pressure, or damage. You could leave it in the rain, drop it, and use it for a long time without destroying it.

Invent Your Own Material

Now that you know so much about materials, it's time to design your own! Describe the problem your material solves, draw what it looks like, and give it an interesting name.

 An **invention** is something humans create to solve problems or make life more fun! Think about how your material might solve a problem or make life more fun.

Name your invention:

Describe the problem it solves and/or how it makes life more fun:

Draw your material and how it will be used:

OFFICIAL TAPPITY ENGINEER!

Draw or tape your picture here.

Tappity Engineer Team Challenge

Answer these questions with your engineering team in class or with the on-demand lesson and become an official Tappity Engineer!

1. True or false
Paper is a durable material.

2. True or false
Metal is a good conductor of heat.

3. True or false
Humans invent because it's easy.

4. True or false
A house built out of cheese in a desert would be strong and durable.

5. True or false
These are all properties of materials: strength, durability, how easily it melts, color, and transparency.

Strong & Durable Materials Review

Circle the correct material for each prompt.

Circle the strongest material:

Circle the most durable material:

Circle the strongest AND most durable material

27

Q: What makes the Great Pyramid of Giza so strong?

A: The Great Pyramid of Giza is so strong and durable that it has lasted for thousands of years and will last for many thousands more! It is very strong because it's built like a giant puzzle with really heavy stone blocks that fit together perfectly. It also has a large and wide base, which helps it stay balanced and not tip over.

Build a Strong Paper Structure

Based on what you learned, build a strong structure and then have a friend or parent test its strength.

 Materials needed for this activity: 20+ paper index cards. Objects like a book or apple to test how much weight your structure can hold.

Step 1
15-30 mins

Use index cards to build a strong structure that can hold the weight of a book, an apple, or other objects around your house.

Step 2
5 mins

Invite a parent or friend to test your structure's strength by putting increasingly heavier objects on it.

Step 3
15-30 mins

Make improvements to your structure and repeat step 2. Continue for as long as you can think of improvements!

Q: What do plants need to survive?

A: Plants need sunlight to make their own food in a process called photosynthesis. They also need water and nutrient-rich soil to grow well.

Design a Greenhouse

Brainstorm and draw your greenhouse design below. Consider what plants need and the building materials you would use when designing.

 A **greenhouse** is a see-through structure where we grow and protect plants indoors. It's made of glass or plastic, and keeps plants warm so they can grow when it's cold outside.

Draw your design for a greenhouse:

Parent Review

Discussion questions

1. What does it mean if a material is strong? What does it mean if it's durable? *(Answer: Strong materials can resist heavy impact and absorb large amounts of energy without breaking. Durable materials can withstand wear and tear for a long time.)*

2. What material do you want to invent? What problem does it solve?

3. What would happen if you built a house out of chocolate? How might you make your chocolate house last longer?

Parent sign-off

☑During-Class Pages ☐After-Class Pages ☐Discussion Questions

✕ _____ Parent signature

Don't worry about completing activities if they aren't useful/doable for your family. Your child can always follow along with them in our video recordings.

Chapter 3
Innovative Plants

📝 Chapter Summary

In this chapter, students will look at plants and seeds from the perspective of an engineer in order to unravel the reasons behind their unique characteristics! We'll run an experiment to discover how the same tree species can end up on two distant islands and how seeds have adapted for optimal dispersal. Get ready to be inspired by the ingenious structures and designs of the natural world, and learn how they can spark innovative engineering ideas!

Next Generation Science Standards covered
2-LS2-2, 2-PS1-1, K-2-ETS1-1, K-2-ETS1-2, K-2-ETS1-3

Javan Seed

Maple Seed

Koa Seed

How Do Trees Travel?

Follow along with the experiment in class or on-demand video lesson.

Some plant seeds are like tiny airplanes and helicopters, designed to fly, so they can grow away from the parent plant and get resources like sun light!

Add your hypothesis. A hypothesis is an educated guess.

Draw the path each seed takes through the air.

Javan Seed Path

Maple Seed Path

Koa Seed Path

Seed Dispersal Methods

Circle the images that represent the ways seeds can disperse.

Seed dispersal is how plants send their seeds away to different places, so new plants can grow far from the parent plant.

Tappity Trivia Challenge

Answer these questions in class with your team or with Haley in the on-demand video lesson.

1. True or false

The scientific phrase for describing how plants spread their seeds is known as "seed dispersal".

2. True or false

The tree that traveled from Hawaii to Réunion Island is known as the Coconut tree.

3. True or false

Coconuts and coco de mer rely on the wind and animals to disperse their seeds.

Seed Dispersal

Match the seeds or pods to how they get dispersed, and explain why you think they travel in that particular way.

Mango Seed

Why? It tastes good, so animals want to eat it.

Dandelion Seed

Why?

Coconut Seed

Why?

Cherry Seed

Why?

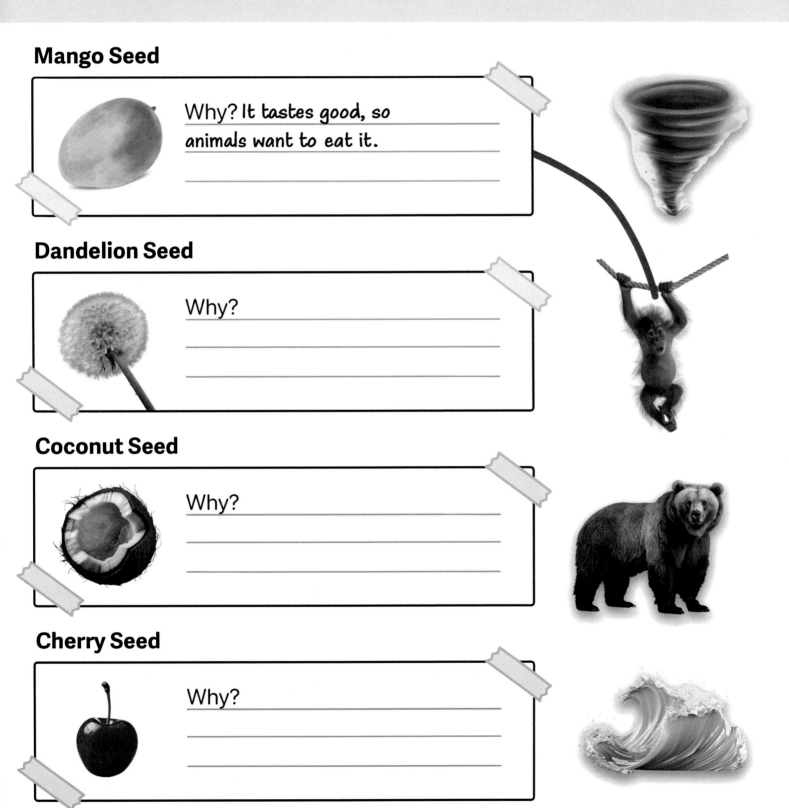

Q: True or false. Ecballium elaterium can shoot their seeds up to 20 feet

True! The Ecballium plant is also known as the "squirting cucumber" because it shoots its seeds out like a water gun. When the pod is filled with too much pressure, it blasts out its seeds, so the seeds can grow in a new area without competing with the parent plant.

Invent Your Own Seed

Now that you know what makes a seed succesful, let's use your engineering mind to design your own seed! Think about what materials you would use, what shape it would be, how it breaks apart (like pinecones), how it protects itself from water, its taste, etc. Get creative!

Name your new seed:

Describe your seed (does it fly, float, taste good, etc):

Draw what your seed looks like and label its features:

Q: True or false. This is a real plane.

False, it's actually a model. A model is a simpler version of something complicated used to understand complicated things. NASA uses wind tunnels to study aerodynamics, which is all about how air moves around things like planes and rockets. When they test models like this plane in the wind tunnel, NASA can make better and safer flying machines for everyone!

Model Seed Test Experiment

Cut out these model seed pods and fold them into shape. Cut on the solid lines, fold on the dotted lines, and place a paper clip to act as the seed. Drop them from up high to see how they fly.

 A scientific model is like a mini-version of something really big or complicated. It helps scientists understand how things work in the real world, kind of like how toy cars can help you understand how real cars move and turn!

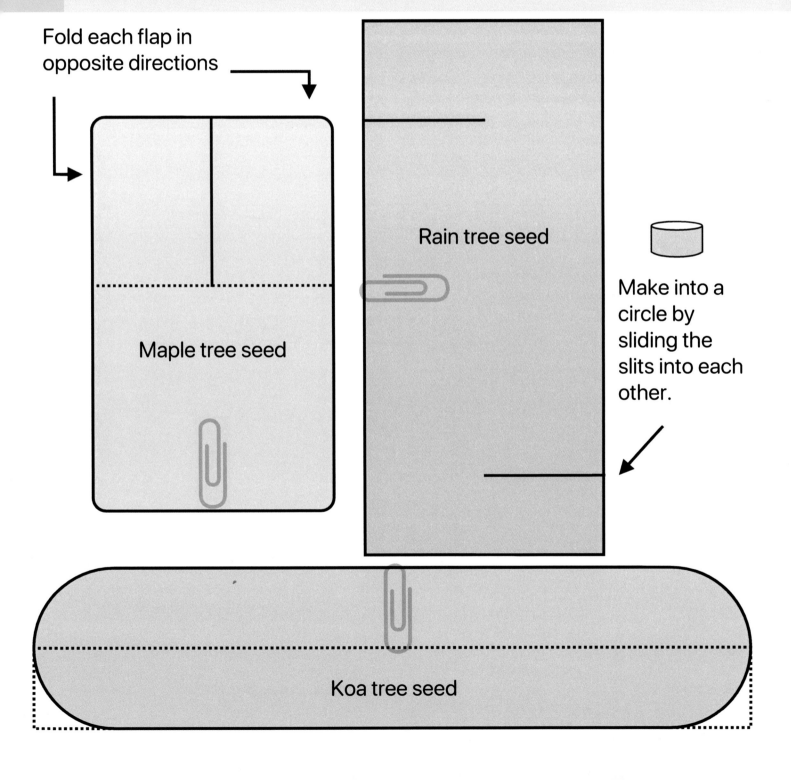

Fold each flap in opposite directions

Maple tree seed

Rain tree seed

Make into a circle by sliding the slits into each other.

Koa tree seed

Parent Review

🗨 Discussion questions

1) What does the scientific phrase "seed dispersal" mean? *(Answer: How plant seeds spread, often by wind, water, or animals.)*

2) What is animal seed dispersal? *(Answer: Animal seed dispersal is when animals help plants spread their seeds by eating the fruit and later dropping the seeds in new locations in their poop.)*

3) Why do coconuts have a thick shell? *(Answer: The thick shell helps it float and survive the salt in the ocean.)*

Parent sign-off

☑ During-Class Pages ☐ After-Class Pages ☐ Discussion Questions

✕ _____ Parent signature

💡 Don't worry about completing activities if they aren't useful/doable for your family. Your child can always follow along with them in our video recordings.

Chapter 4

The Power of Time and Water

📝 Chapter Summary

In this chapter, students delve into the world of erosion to learn how various land formations are created. Through two hands-on experiments, students will discover how water shapes canyons and apply their engineering knowledge from earlier in the course to develop ways to prevent landslides, just as real scientists do. This class takes a deep dive into the power of water and the materials used to mitigate natural disasters.

Next Generation Science Standards covered
K-2-ETS1-2, K-2-ETS1-1, 2-PS1-2, 2-ESS2-1, 2-ESS2-2

The Schleier waterfall in Austria

Waterflow

Draw where water could form rivers and lakes.

 Glacial lakes form when glaciers melt, leaving behind carved-out basins that fill with water.
Tectonic lakes are created when Earth's crust shifts, forming depressions that collect water.

During the experiment, take note of the landforms that are emerging in the mountain erosion model.

Earth's Surface Model Experiment

Follow along with the experiment in class or on-demand video lesson.

 Erosion is when tiny pieces of the Earth's surface are moved from one place to another typically by water or wind. Erosion usually takes a very long time.

Add your hypothesis. A hypothesis is guess based on what you know.

Rainfall 1

Rainfall 2

Rainfall 3

Rainfall 4

Antelope Canyon in Arizona

Tappity Trivia Challenge

Answer these questions in class with your team or with Haley in the on-demand video lesson.

1. True or false
The image on the ← left is an example of erosion.

2. True or false
Erosion usually happens very fast.

3. Circle the hill that is more likely to have landslides.

4. True or false
It's impossible to prevent landslides.

Q: True or false. You can find examples of erosion everywhere.

Erosion is Earth's way of reshaping itself, and it's happening everywhere—even in your backyard, the nearby creek, or the park. Every time it rains, water moves soil around, changing the landscape over time. You can be an explorer and look for signs of erosion wherever you go; you'll be amazed at what you can find!

Spot the Erosion

Circle at least 3 examples of erosion in the picture below. Then, draw arrows showing the direction of water flowing over each surface.

Q: True or false. Plateaus like this one cover close to 20% of Earth's surface.

True! Plateaus cover about 18% of the Earth's land surface. A plateau is an elevated area with more or less leveled land on top. They are also called high plains or tablelands.

Label the Landforms

Write the type of landform below each image.

 A landform is a natural feature on Earth's surface created by various geological processes and shaped by the elements including the wind, water, and ice.

Landforms

Mountains	Canyon	Plain
Plateau	Hills	Valley

Plateau

Erosion & Landform Adventure

Go outside, and document erosion and landforms.

Step 1

Choose an adventure. This can be a walk in your neighborhood, backyard, or a local hiking spot.

Step 2

On your adventure, take pictures of erosion or any landforms that you observe.

Step 3

On the next page, draw and describe examples of erosion and land forms that you observed on your hike.

 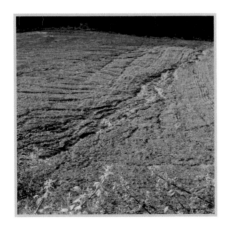 

Draw erosion or landform

Describe what you saw and how you think it formed.

Draw erosion or landform

Describe what you saw and how you think it formed.

Draw erosion or landform

Describe what you saw and how you think it formed.

Parent Review

Discussion questions

1. If you floated down a river long enough, where would you end up? *(Answer: Usually in a lake, sea, or ocean.)*

2. What is your favorite landform and why? (e.g. mountains, canyons, plains, etc)

3. How does water shape the Earth's surface? Is it fast? *(Answer: Water hits Earth's surface and moves small pieces of dirt and rock around. Over long periods of time this makes big changes to Earth's surface and create all sorts of amazing land formations.)*

Parent sign-off

☑ During Class-Pages ☐ After-Class Pages ☐ Discussion Questions

✕ _____ Parent signature

💡 Don't worry about completing activities if they aren't useful/doable for your family. Your child can always follow along with them in our video recordings.

Chapter 5
Animal Architects

📝 Chapter Summary

In this chapter, we're going on a journey to explore the animal kingdom and learn about how animals are sorted into groups. Our focus will be on birds, those amazing aviators, and discover what makes each kind of bird unique. But we won't just watch; we'll also use our science and engineering skills to create a special bird feeder just for one type of bird. It's a fun trip where we use science and engineering to unlock the secrets of nature!

Next Generation Science Standards covered
2-LS4-1, K-2-ETS1-1, K-2-ETS1-2, K-2-ETS1-3

Animal Grouping

Name each animal group.

Vertebrates are animals with a spine (backbone). Scientists categorized them into 5 large groups: fish, mammals, reptiles, birds, and amphibians.

Invertebrates
(No spine)

Vertebrates
(Has a spine)

Bird Species

Circle the parts that make a bird unique from other animals.

 Biodiversity is the range of different kinds of living things you can find in one place, from plants and animals to even tiny microbes.

What & How Birds Eat

Identify what each bird eats and what bird feeder it prefers.

Jays

Woodpeckers

Finches

Cardinals

Eagles

Hummingbirds

68

Bird Feeder Design Activity (Part 1)
Choose the type of bird you'll feed with your bird feeder.

What type of bird are you making your bird feeder for?

What does your bird eat?

How does your bird stand when it eats?

How will you protect your bird feeder from predators like cats?

Bird Feeder Design Activity (Part 2)

Draw two bird feeder designs based on your problem statement (part 1).

Make sure to include where food will be placed and where birds will stand. Also, think about how you can protect the feeder from cats or other predators. Consider the materials on the previous page.

Bird feeder idea 1

Bird feeder idea 2

Use these homemade bird feeders as inspiration for creating your own!

Bird Feeder Design Activity (Part 3)

Build your bird feeder. Bring your bird feeder to the final trivia class if you want to share it with Haley and your teammates.

 You can bring any activity or project you completed as part of this course to your final trivia class. The first 10 minutes will be dedicated to celebrating your creations!

Step 1

Choose one of your bird feeder designs and create a prototype or model of it.

Step 2

Collect materials from around your house to create the bird feeder.

Step 3

Build your bird feeder. Make sure there is room for the birds to stand and a place for food that birds can reach. Use the image on the previous page for inspiration.

Step 4

Depending on your weather, place your bird feeder somewhere outside, like your backyard.

Step 5

Observe if birds come to your bird feeder. What type of birds are they?

Q: True or false. These are living animals, not plants.

True! These animals are called Christmas Tree Worms! These colorful invertebrates (animals without a spine) look like Christmas trees, but they're more than just eye candy. Those feathery "branches" are their personal fishing nets, snagging plankton from the water.

Circle the Invertebrates

Remember invertebrates have no bones.

Q: True or false. There are ~50,000 species of butterflies.

False! There are over 180,000 types of butterflies!

Tappity Trivia Challenge

Review what you learned in this chapter with some fun trivia!

1. True or false

Fish, Mammals, Birds, Reptiles, and Amphibians are all invertebrates.

2. Circle the right answer

A butterfly is...
a. A bird, because it has wings and can fly
b. A reptile, because it lays eggs
c. An invertebrate, because it doesn't have bones
d. None of the above

3. Circle the bird feeder that is made for a woodpecker.

4. True or false

All birds eat the same food.

Parent Review

🗨 Discussion questions

1. What is an example of a vertebrate? *(Answer: Any animal with a spine.)*

2. What type of bird would you like to attract and how would you design a bird feeder to do that?

3. Why do you think different types of birds have different beaks? *(Answer: To help them eat specific types of food they like.)*

Parent sign-off

☑ During-Class Pages ☐ After-Class Pages ☐ Discussion Questions

✕ _____ Parent signature

💡 Don't worry about completing activities if they aren't useful/doable for your family. Your child can always follow along with them in our video recordings.

Chapter 6

Assessment & Beyond

 Chapter Summary

Get ready for a unique and fun assessment in this final chapter. We're reviewing all the important ideas from the course--with a twist! Many questions are open-ended (with more than one right answer) and designed to kickstart lively discussion. Students will review, think, and see their learning journey in a whole new light. End the course on a high note--full of fun and reflection!

Engineering & Invention

Follow along in class, with the on-demand video, or on your own.

1. Inventing

Oliver: "Inventing is when you do a really hard experiment."

Mathilda: "Inventing is when you solve a problem and improve people's lives."

Nathan: "Inventing is when you create something that is fun."

Who do you agree with and why?

_____

_____

_____

2. Label each state of matter (solid, liquid, gas)

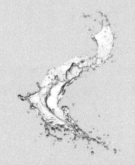

_____ 　　 _____ 　　 _____

82

3. Properties of materials

 **Oliver:** "Different materials help solve different problems depending on their properties."

 **Mathilda:** "The most important property of material is how strong it is"

 **Nathan:** "The most important property of a material is how flexible it is"

Who do you agree with and why?

_____

_____

_____

4. This image is an example of what? (circle your answer)

a. A model
b. An illustration
c. An experiment
d. A hypothesis

Plants & Seeds

Follow along in class, with the on-demand video, or on your own.

1. Seed dispersal: Look at the three seeds below. Which one travels by water, which one by wind, and which one by animals? Label each one.

_____   _____   _____

2. True or false
Seeds disperse away from parent plants so they don't compete for resources like sunlight.

3. If you planted a cactus in the forest, the cactus would probably...

a. Grow really well.
b. Get too much light.
c. Get too much water and not enough light
d. Be eaten by the animals there.

Q: True or false. Some pine cone species need fire to grow.

True! Some pine cones, like the Lodgepole and Jack Pine, are like nature's safes. They lock up their seeds with a resin that only melts in a fire. Once a fire happens, boom! The seeds are free and fall into the fresh soil, helping new trees grow. It's nature's clever way of bouncing back after a fire. Simple, but pretty smart, don't you think?

Erosion & Landforms

Follow along in class, with the on-demand video, or on your own.

1. **If it never rained, would Earth look different? Explain.**

_____

_____

_____

_____

2. **True or false**
Rivers start in high places and flow to lower places.

3. **True or false**
Water is not powerful.

4. **Circle the images that are examples of erosion**

Q: True or false. The astronaut footprint on the moon will probably last millions of years.

True! On Earth, your footprints in the sand don't last, thanks to wind and waves. On the Moon? Different story—no air, no wind. Those Apollo footprints could stick around for millions of years. While the moon gets hit by tiny space rocks and experiences "moonquakes," they don't change the surface too much. Bottom line: Those lunar footprints are about as permanent as you can get!

Animals & Classification

Follow along in class, with the on-demand video, or on your own.

1. Scientific method

Nathan thinks if he makes a bird feeder that requires a bird to have a long beak and for it to atttach itself in order to feed, it will attract woodpeckers.

What do scientists call this guess that Billy has made?

a. A taxonomy
b. An experiment
c. A hypothesis
d. A random idea

2. If you were trying to find out what type of food a bird eats, which body parts would you look at in order to make a guess and why?

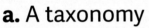

_____

_____

_____

_____

_____

_____

_____

_____

3. A new species is discovered! How should we figure out what group it belongs to?

Oliver: "We should look at the outside of the animal to see if it looks like a fish or something else."

Mathilda: "We should look at the inside of the animal to see if it has bones".

Nathan: "We need to look at both the inside and outside to figure out which group it is in."

Who do you agree with and why?

_____

_____

_____

4. A fly is...

a. A reptile, because it lays eggs
b. An invertebrate, because it doesn't have bones
c. A bird, because it has wings and can fly
d. None of the above

Badge Collection

Each month, we'll send you the badges you've earned in this course. Use this page to collect and proudly display all your badges!

Secret Mission

Secret Mission Alert! Haley has scattered the objects shown below throughout this book. Your mission: Note the page number where you find each object. Once you've located them all, ask a parent to snap a photo of this completed page and email it to haley@tappityapp.com and earn an exclusive badge!